TAMSIN AND THE DEEP

NEILL CAMERON
KATE BROWN

Tamsin and the Deep
is a
DAVID FICKLING BOOK

First published in Great Britain in 2016 by
David Fickling Books,
31 Beaumont Street,
Oxford, OX1 2NP
www.davidficklingbooks.com

978-1-910200-77-3

1 3 5 7 9 10 8 6 4 2

David Fickling Books supports the Forest Stewardship Council (FSC), the leading international forest certication organisation.
All our titles that are printed on Greenpeace-approved FSC-certied paper carry the FSC logo.

MIX
Paper from
responsible sources
FSC
www.fsc.org   FSC® C020872

DAVID FICKLING BOOKS Reg. No. 8340307

A CIP catalogue record for this book
is available from the British Library.

Printed and bound in Great Britain
by Polestar Stones.

Contents

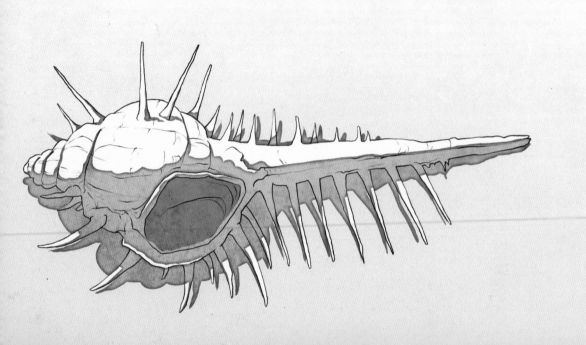

6

TAMSIN!

SHAAAAWF!!

TAMSIN...!!

11

12

The EXTREMELY Secret Diary of Tamsin Thomas (10)

FRIDAY, NOVEMBER 27TH.

DEAR DIARY:
IT HAS BEEN A REALLY WEIRD WEEK.

SO APPARENTLY I SANK WHEN I WAS BODYBOARDING AND EVERYONE THOUGHT I WAS DROWNED AND I WASN'T BUT WHEN I CAME BACK IT WAS A MONTH LATER.

THE POLICE CAME, AND THERE WAS A LADY WHO WAS A COUNSELLOR.

OR A COUNCILLOR?

ONE OF THOSE.

THEY ALL WANTED TO KNOW THE SAME THING.

WHERE HAVE YOU BEEN?

AND I TOLD THEM ALL THE SAME THING.

...I DON'T REMEMBER.

WHICH IS TRUE.

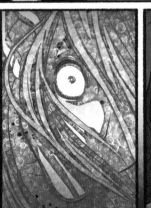

MOSTLY.

13

...SHOULD HAVE NEVER BEEN OUT THERE IN THE FIRST PLACE. AT THIS TIME OF YEAR!

...AND ON HER OWN!

MUM'S IN A BIT OF A STATE, STILL.

COME HERE! COME HERE AND GIVE ME A HUG!

MUUUM! YOU'VE NOT STOPPED SINCE I GOT BACK!

NO, AND I'M NEVER GOING TO, EITHER.

...SOB SOB SNFFF SOB...

MUUUUM!

I TELL HER I'M FINE.

I WISH SHE WASN'T SO UPSET.

I GUESS IT'S BECAUSE OF WHAT HAPPENED TO DAD.

14

AND SOMETIMES
I'M BACK IN THE WATER.

AND I CAN'T GET
TO THE SURFACE,
AND I THINK I'M GOING
TO DROWN.

AND THEN I REALISE,
IT ISN'T ME DROWNING.

IT'S MORGAN.

AND THEN
I WAKE UP.

AHHHHH!!!

...WAIT,
WHAT?

24

26

27

HEY, GUYS. WHAT'S UP?

SORRY, MORGAN - CAN'T TALK! THEY JUST CALLED OUR HEAT!

SUCKS YOU COULDN'T ENTER!

SUCKS FOR YOU!

YES, IT DOES.

THANKS.

YOU LOOK SAD.

WHAT?

ME?

I'M JUST...

...WHAT?

YOUR FRIENDS ARE ENTERING THE CONTEST, HUH? THAT'S COOL.

HUH. THOSE IDIOTS?

THEY SUCK. I'M LIKE TEN TIMES A BETTER SURFER THAN THOSE GUYS.

SHAME YOU'RE NOT ENTERING, THEN.

THAT WOULD BE SO COOL.

UM...

...WELL...

I...

I PROMISED TAMSIN!

BUT TAMSIN'S JUST BEING A WEIRDO.

BUT I DID PROMISE.

BUT GIRL!

AH, STUFF IT. I WILL ENTER!

...I CAN BORROW A BOARD AND A WETSUIT OFF CRAIG, THAT GUY ALWAYS PIKES OUT...

AND WHAT'S MORE, I'LL WIN!

UM, MAYBE SEE YOU AFTER?

OH, DEFINITELY.

CATCH YOU LATER.

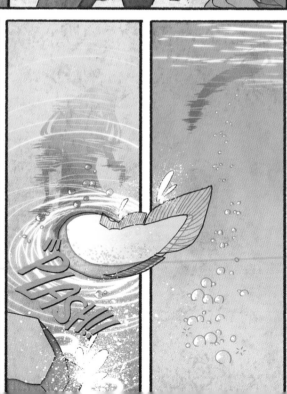

UM.

WHOOOSH!!!

WAH!

WHAT... WHAT WAS THAT?

THEY'RE CALLED *UNDINES.* KIND OF OCEAN NYMPHS, BASICALLY. GREEDY LITTLE BEGGARS.

MOST PEOPLE CAN'T SEE 'EM, OR JUST MISTAKE 'EM FOR GULLS.

HUH. HOW COME I COULD SEE IT?

WELL, THAT'S REALLY THE QUESTION, ISN'T IT?

AAAH! TALKING BLACKBIRD!

I'M A *CHOUGH,* THANK YOU VERY MUCH.

YOU KNOW, YOU SHOULD REALLY TELL YOUR BROTHER TO STAY AWAY FROM THE WATER.

...WHAT?

37

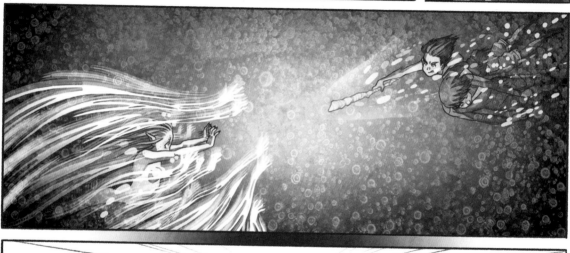

FWOOOSHH!!!

CHAPTER 3
FAMILY
MYTHOLOGY

I'M HOOOME!

MORGAN? TAMSIN?

HELLOOO?

ANYONE?

OH, WHERE HAVE THEY GOT TO NOW?

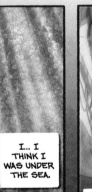

DARK.

I WAS... IN A DARK PLACE.

I... I THINK I WAS UNDER THE SEA.

BUT THERE'S A PLACE DOWN THERE - A SECRET PLACE.

AND SOMETHING WAS CHASING ME. I REACHED OUT FOR... I DON'T KNOW...

...FOR ANYTHING, TO DEFEND MYSELF. AND THEN...

EVERYTHING WENT WHITE.

...THAT'S IT? THAT'S *RUBBISH!*

COME ON, YOU MUST REMEMBER MORE THAN THAT. YOU WERE GONE FOR A MONTH.

I CAN'T HELP IT! IT'S ALL... HAZY.

I'VE *BEEN* THINKING ABOUT IT, TRYING TO PIECE IT TOGETHER, AND I FIGURE...

THAT *THING* MUST HAVE GRABBED ME.

YOU MEAN, THE...

...I CAN'T EVEN BRING MYSELF TO SAY IT, IT SOUNDS SO STUPID...

...THE *MERMAID?*

...THE *MERMAID.*

...MAN. MERMAIDS.

WHAT THE ACTUAL **FLIP.**

...ANYWAY, SHE *TOOK* ME SOMEWHERE. AND... WHEREVER IT WAS, *TIME* MUST WORK FUNNY THERE.

BECAUSE IT ONLY FELT LIKE, I DUNNO, A FEW *HOURS* FOR ME.

AND I MUST HAVE MANAGED TO ESCAPE, AND SOMEHOW... IT WAS BECAUSE I FOUND *THIS.*

IT'S BECAUSE OF LUCKY STICK.

...CAN I HAVE A *GO?*

UMMMM..

I DUNNO...

OH, GO ON.
I'LL BE CAREFUL
WITH IT!

ALL RIGHT,
BUT JUST FOR
A MINUTE.

OH, MAN.
MAGIC STICK!

I'M GOING TO
FLY AROUND AND
SHOOT FIREBALLS
AND...

AND...

IT'S NOT
DOING
ANYTHING!

TAMSIN!
WHY ISN'T
IT DOING
ANYTHING?

UM.

...MAYBE IT
ONLY WORKS
FOR ME?

TYPICAL!

YOU GET A
COOL AWESOME
MAGIC STICK,
AND I GET A MERMAID
FOR A STALKER!

THIS IS
SO UNFAIR!

BAMF!

MORGAN,
WAIT!

AH, LET
HIM GO.

48

HA HA HA! I CAUGHT YOU!

OKAY, SO I GET TO ASK YOU ANOTHER QUESTION!

NO, FIRST I ASK YOU ONE. THAT'S THE RULES.

YOUR DAD.

WHAT DO YOU REMEMBER ABOUT YOUR DAD?

WHAT? NO, I... NO.

COME ON, PLAY THE GAME.

I DON'T WANT TO TALK ABOUT MY DAD WITH A WEIRD TALKING BIRD.

AND ANYWAY, I CAN'T REMEMBER ANYTHING.

HE WAS A FISHERMAN. I DUNNO. I WAS ONLY A BABY WHEN... WHEN HE...

I...

...IT WAS THE NIGHT HIS SHIP WENT DOWN.

IT WAS JUST A MOMENT, BUT...

HE WAS THERE.

HE WAS IN MY ROOM, AND HE SMILED AT ME.

AND THEN HE WAS GONE.

BUT IT'S IMPOSSIBLE –

I CAN'T REMEMBER THAT, I WAS TOO LITTLE. AND ANYWAY...

...YES?

51

Once, long ago, there lived in these parts a man named Lutey.

He was a beachcomber, a farmer, and, on occasion, a smuggler. A Cornishman, in short.

One fine morning he was out walking on the beach with his dog, Venture...

...when he saw a sight that fair near stopped his heart.

Sitting on the edge of a rock pool, weeping — a woman.

The most beautiful woman he'd ever seen...

WAAAAIT A MINUTE.

WHAT KIND OF A STORY IS THIS?

COR! KIDS TODAY AND THEIR ATTENTION SPANS.

JUST LET ME TELL IT, WILL YOU?

Lutey wanted to help the lass, but did not wish to give her fear. Carefully, he drew near...

When something glinting 'neath the water caught his eye.

A mermaid! She gasped with fright when she saw him.

Please, sir! she said, I beg ye, do me no harm!

I wish ye no harm, miss, said Lutey, I never beheld such a wondrous creature. But tell me, why are ye crying?

And so the mermaid explained her plight. She'd been at play in the surf with some of her kind.

As she sat, combing her hair, she'd not taken sight of the tide going out...

And now, I cannot get back to the sea, and I will surely die here!

I cannot have that, said Lutey, and with that he took her in his arms and carried her out into the surf.

How can I ever repay ye, kind sir? asked the mermaid, Just name your reward, and it is yours. Anything your heart desires. Anything.

THIS STORY BETTER NOT BE ABOUT TO GET GROSS.

WOULD YOU JUST LET ME FINISH?!

54

...TO YOU.

NO... THAT'S NOT...

IS THAT WHY I SEE WEIRD STUFF?

AND YOU'VE SEEN THEM ALL YOUR LIFE, HAVEN'T YOU? OUT THE CORNER OF YOUR EYE. SEEN THE THINGS THAT NO ONE ELSE COULD SEE.

EVEN IF YOU DIDN'T KNOW EXACTLY WHAT THEY WERE.

EVEN IF YOU DIDN'T WANT TO SEE THEM.

THE PISKEYS, THE BROWNIES, THE BUCCAS AND THE KNOCKERS.

ALL THE CREATURES OF THE HIDDEN WORLD.

LIKE THOSE ONES BEHIND YOU, FOR EXAMPLE.

WHAT?

WHACK!!

SO ANYWAY, WHERE WAS I?

WHACK!!

OH, YEAH. THE MERMAID GAVE OLD LUTEY HER COMB...

ARE YOU KIDDING ME?

YOU'RE STILL TELLING YOUR DUMB STORY?

I AM KIND OF BUSY HERE!

WELL, MULTI-TASK. I'M JUST GETTING TO THE GOOD BIT.

It seemed the mermaid had grown fond of Lutey, and was reluctant to let him go.

Come with me, My Love,

she whispered,

and dwell with me, beneath the sea.

And she spoke to him of the beauty there,

of jewel-encrusted caverns, and treasure, and how he would never grow old there and never die.

Lutey was entranced, and was about to consent, when...

Ruff!

Ruff!

Ruff!

He heard his dog upon the shore, and in an instant the spell was broken.

Thank ye, fair miss,

he said,

but I have a life, and a family, on the land. I cannot go with ye.

Oh, I think you can.

58

Lutey went about his life, but he never forgot the creature.

And then, nine years later, as he was out fishing one day...

She returned for him, and called to him again...

And took him down with her, to the deep.

And return she has, every nine years since.

Every time, claiming one of his descendants and dragging them down to a watery grave.

And now it's time again, and she's coming back. For the last male child of Lutey's line. For...

MORGAN!

BUT I CAN STOP IT THOUGH, RIGHT? I CAN STOP HER?

...HELLO?

SLAMMM!!

TAMSIN?
IS THAT
YOU?

MORGAN!

WHAT?

...AND NEXT
ON ITVI
IT'S THE
X FACTOR...

TAMSIN,
GOODNESS -
YOU'RE SOAKING
WET!

I WILL
PROTECT YOU,
MORGAN!

GET
OFF ME YOU
UNBELIEVABLE
WEIRDO!

TAMSIN,
WHAT'S GOT
INTO YOU?

APART FROM
MENTAL
ILLNESS?

WE'RE
SAFE HERE.
I'LL PROTECT
YOU.

SAFE AT
HOME.

SAFE AT
HOME.

SAFE AT...

KABHOOM!

IT JUST LOOKS LIKE AN ORDINARY SEA SHELL... BUT THERE'S SOMETHING ELSE THERE.

RUFF?

STORE 1

I CAN SENSE IT... THERE'S POWER THERE. THERE'S... MAGIC.

IF I CAN JUST FIGURE OUT HOW TO UN-MAGIC IT...

...I COULD BREAK THE CURSE! I COULD SAVE MORGAN! I COULD...

TAMSIN?

NOTHING!

STORE 1

TAMSIN? ARE YOU OKAY?

WHAT? NOTHING! I MEAN... YES?

SORRY ABOUT THIS, LOVE. WE CAN GET OFF HOME SOON, AGNES JUST NEEDED SOME EXTRA COVER WHILE TERRY'S DOWN WITH SHINGLES.

IT'S FINE, I'M... DOING MY HOMEWORK.

WHERE'S MORGAN, THOUGH?

HOW COME HE DOESN'T HAVE TO HANG OUT HERE?

TOLD 'EM, I DID. TOLD 'EM ALL.

KIDS TODAY. THEY JUST DON'T LISTEN.

AHA!

RUN!

RUFF!!! RUFF!!

RUFF!!!

SOMETHING'S HAPPENING OUT THERE...

MORGAN...!

Mermaid's Res

MROOAAARR!!!

YEAH, YOU **BETTER** RUN!

WAH!

WHERE'S MORGAN? WAS HE WITH YOU?

MONSTERS!

THERE WERE **MONSTERS!**

THEY'RE GOING!

BACK INTO THE **SEA!**

MORGAN... THEY'VE GOT MORGAN...

WHAT?!

THE MONSTERS... THEY **TOOK** HIM...

OH NO YOU DON'T.

TAMSIN!

SSSSSS! YOU.

LET THEM ALL GO, YOU WITCH.

HOW EVER YOU'RE DOING IT, THIS WHOLE... DEAL, THIS COVENANT.

IT'S OVER. THE DEAL'S OFF.

HAVE YOUR STUPID COMB BACK.

YOU HAVE NO POWER TO BREAK THE COVENANT, CHILD!

WHY ARE YOU EVEN HERE?

WHY AM I EVEN HERE? YOU STARTED THIS ALL, WHEN YOU TOOK ME!

YOU STEAL THE MENFOLK OR WHATEVER - WHY DID YOU TAKE ME?

I...

...THE MAGICKS WERE CONFUSED. YOU WERE BOTH IN THE WATER.

AND YOU SO CLOSELY RESEMBLE A MALE CHILD.

YOU...

YOU THOUGHT I WAS A BOY?!

THE END

TAMSIN THOMAS WILL RETURN IN...

TAMSIN AND THE DARK

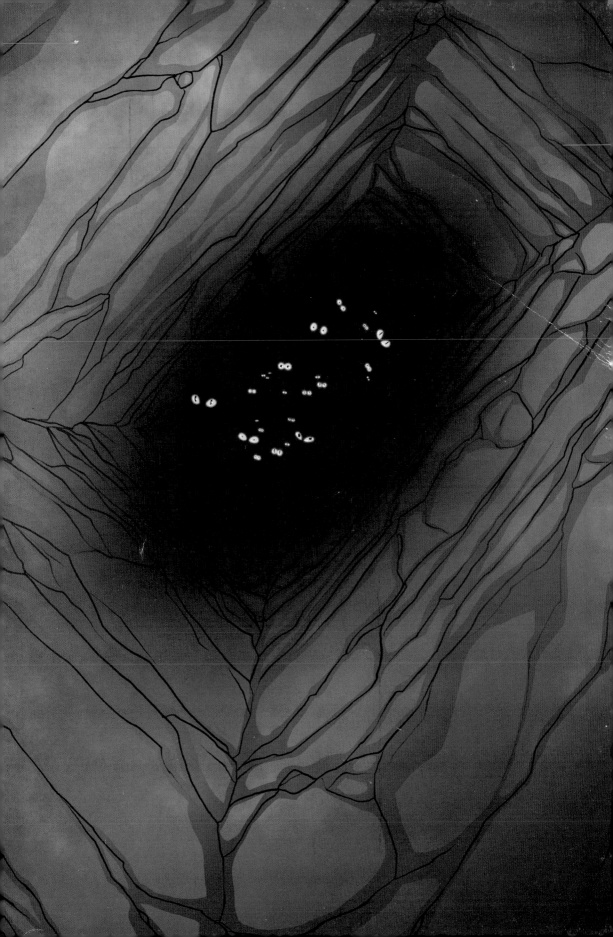